THE LAND BEFORE YOGHURT

ALSO BY ALISTAIR ROBINSON

Stereograms of the Dead, Red Squirrel Press, 2009
South of Souter, Sand, 2003
Sunderland Empire, A Centenary History, Tempus, 2006
Sunderland, Wear Books, 2006
Sunderland Empire, A History of the Theatre and its Stars, 2000

THE LAND
BEFORE YOGHURT

Poems

Alistair Robinson

RED SQUIRREL PRESS

First published in the UK in 2014 by
Red Squirrel Press
www.redsquirrelpress.com

Red Squirrel Press is distributed by Central Books
and represented by Inpress Ltd.
www.inpressbooks.co.uk

Designed and typeset by Gerry Cambridge
gerry.cambridge@btinternet.com
Set in Bembo Book and Requiem

A CIP catalogue record is available from the British Library.

ISBN: 978 1 906700 85 0

Printed by Martins the Printers
www.martins-the-printers.co.uk

Contents

For Laura, Jasmine,
Rosie and Nina

Without You

Never thought I'd say it,
but I miss you.
It's kind of quiet round here
without you.

I'd be the first to admit it:
we didn't always get on.
We didn't work to the same system.
It was a pain to hide my lunch
in the oven when I went to
answer the door.
I could no longer
leave dishes on the drainer.
And I objected to you
nipping my legs
when I sat down to eat.

But we kind of accepted
each other.

Of course, I knew it couldn't last:
I'd left a space for you
next to the stiff-legged moth
on the windowsill. But
you're not even there.

I miss you, fly.

Life's Rich Tapestry

I know I probably shouldn't grumble—
and it does match the three-piece—
but sometimes, when they're working in
all those rich colours, or when they've just
nipped out for some more gold leaf,
I can't help but think that
it would be nicer if
it was just
a little plainer.

Don't Look Too Loud

Sometimes I think I've discovered the secret
of sleep. Not the sleep that comes happily,
but the sort that needs looking for in dark corners
of the night.

It can be found like commonplace hidden things
can be found: by not looking for it.
You have to picture something—preferably
somewhere—that has nothing to do with sleep, say,
a small fishing port on the Lincolnshire coast, or,
better still, a small fishing port on the Shropshire
coast, for Shropshire has no coast. This

is the kind of nonsense sleep likes. And then,
to make your looking even less obvious,
you have to avert your gaze behind
its drawn curtain of skin
and look up as if in awe at a statue of a saint
or a mountain peak that has just emerged from cloud.
But you mustn't look too loud.

A Love Story

They are the saddest couple, Lud
and his dog. They've only been together
a couple of weeks and now she won't leave
her butt alone. Can't resist the urge to spin round and put
her tongue there.

In the shed Lud is sad. I feel for him.
He's just got off the phone to the breeder
and has decided not to send the dog back yet.
They'll put her down if she doesn't snap
out of it, he says. Lud has already
spent £160 at the vets but is prepared
to give it one more go. He's resolved
to bathe her teats.

'Women have problems down there,' he reasons.
I draw on my experience of such people.
'Why not run a hot bath and get some
scented candles?' I say. Lud runs with it, says he'll
put some panpipes on the stereo. If that doesn't work
he'll be the one who decides if she has to be
put to sleep.

Now he's out for a walk with her. I see this bull
terrier in a new light. She has a certain
something. As they cross the road to the park
her head tries to reach her haunches. Lud
gives her a quick flick of a stick.

Superstitions*

i.

Knees

Almost as much can be gleaned
about a person's character from
their knees as from their face.

A person with short fat knees
is dim-witted and intemperate, while
those with long knees may well have
'artist's knees' but be foolish with money.

Persons with long fore-knees are
to be mistrusted. The right fore-knee
is sometimes called the 'poison knee' and
is thought to be venomous, so should never be used

to rub ointment into a wound, although
it may be used to rub spittle on to
ringworm patches. And it's a good idea
to cross your knees while telling a white lie or

before embarking on an undertaking, or if you
want to negate the effects of walking
under a ladder. Pointing a knee
at someone is, of course, thought rude and

should especially be discouraged at funerals
for it may lead to the premature death
of the person doing the knee-pointing. Pulling
the knee joints to see if they crack is a test of

love; if they make the correct sound the knee
cracker can be certain that he or she is
in someone else's thoughts. If two people coincidentally
utter the same word together, they should

immediately link both sets of knees and make
a wish. This is sure to come true as long as the
knee-linking is done in complete silence.

ii.

The Budgerigar

The budgerigar, or house petrel
as it is known in parts of Lancashire,
is thought to be a tremendously lucky bird.
If you see one on a Wednesday, and there hasn't
been an outbreak of whooping cough or any
other such pestilence within the past month,
you can be sure to have great fortune.

iii.

Tables

In certain country districts
a table is considered an omen of bad luck.
If, during the night, a table appears in
a previously tableless household,
it is a sure sign that it will rain for forty days.

Either that or the first-born will be complete
in every way except that
its face will be on the back of its head
rather than the front.

with thanks—and apologies—to Cassell's
Dictionary of Superstitions.

The North Dog

What is it with the south?
What happened there?
What happened with me there?
Morning and night we have become
a comedy act on the stage of the park;
I can feel eyes watching us as I try
to gently coax you south
and you, making like a low-limbed
paperweight, pull me by your neck
to the north.

Even when I attempt to head marginally
east-south-east from our house to the grass
you become at one with the pavement.
Even when I attempt to take us marginally
west-south-west to the litter bin to dump
your bag of crap on the way back to the house,
you make me go alone.
What is it with the south?
What happened there?

When, at last I become determined to
take us plumb down the compass
I have to carry you the first five blocks.
'What's happened with your dog?' they ask.
I say: 'The south.
The south happened to my dog.'

Two Poems Inspired by Charles Nègre Photographs

Le Sculpteur Preault (1852)

Perhaps it's just after lunch, a long one.
The sun is on the sculptor's forehead and
he looks well fed, but his mind is on other things.
Perhaps he's still bothered by
the looting of his studio back in '30
or the fact that people don't think he has
the patience to really give form to his imagination.

He looks as though he has been waiting ages for
the thing to go off. He stands tall but both arms must
be aching—one holding his topper behind his back,
the other stuck like Nelson's inside his jacket.
The jacket is smart enough, but his shoes are scuffed.

He's not quite centre-frame. The eye is drawn equally
to an open shutter top-right; rust has run from its screws
and the grimy wall can be seen through the slats—
the whitewash has been greased by bodies
fumbling there in the night. To the left,
there is the entrance to the courtyard of
21 Quai Bourbon and beyond that
everything that the camera didn't see.

Portrait of a Man (1850)

This one's really a picture of a shadow,
a huge mid-afternoon, midwinter shadow which looks like
it has been inked in afterwards.

The shadow is draped over some ancient
doors at the back of the courtyard; the sun
has been working on them since sometime
in the 1600s. It has been helped by dirty fingers and
impatient boots.

There's more of the black stuff packed beneath
the sash of a window and in a deep doorway
and it has been laid in a thick wedge
below the wrought-iron balconies.

Just to give scale to the thing there's
a bloke in a stove-pipe hat and frock coat
propped in the corner.

On the Boulevard Périphérique

It was probably the espresso—
my first-ever espresso—that did it.
Before, I'd only ever had powdered with milk
but the traffic rattling on the fly-over
above the café on the Boulevard Périphérique
didn't help, nor the realisation that
here in France things seemed to happen
earlier. 'Everything starts at about 9.00 back home,'
I explained to Miguel, the formerly Spanish
Frenchman. 'Pretty quiet before then.'

Back in the *camion* cab (this was in the days before
cab freshener), we made for Porte de Clignancourt,
queasily (in my case), and dropped off wine at other
cafés, but mercifully skipped the drinking.
In the attic rooms above the metro stations
and *supermarchés* of the *banlieue* the scruffy laced
curtains concealed French people doing
scruffy laced French stuff, I hoped,
but I didn't share this thought with Miguel,
the formerly Spanish Frenchman, who was
pointing out the radiant Sacre Coeur and
the distant Tour Eiffel.

Back at the depot we had a leisurely *déjeuner*:
fruit, wine, crème caramel, *cervelle* with crisps.
This was also my first horse brains so the cab seemed
rather claustrophobique back on the Boulevard
Périphérique. I was glad of the air after our
last drop-off when we relaxed at the kerb. Miguel,

the increasingly Frenchified Spaniard, lit up
a *Gauloise* untipped and we nodded to passing *piétons*.
Everything seemed restored in the cooling Parisian air as
we pissed against the rear driver-side wheel.

Two Phone Poems

i.

The Concreting

Phone rings.
Wrong number.
Voice says:
It's done.
What's done?
It's done.
What's done?
The concreting.
The concreting's done.

ii.

The Wet Cheese

I phone a cinema in Scotland.
Want to know what's on.
'The Wet Cheese,' says the woman.
'The Wet Cheese?' I say.
'I've never heard of it.'
'Is it a new release?'
'No, it's the Wet Cheese,' says the woman.
'You know,' she says. 'The Wet Cheese.'
'I've really never heard of it,' I say.
'Everybody knows The Wet Cheese,' she says.
'What? Like damp dairy produce?' I say.
'The Wet Cheese!' she says.
'The Wet Cheese!'
'Roald Dahl's The Wet Cheese!'

The Thing on the Roof

You always get that bit wrong, you say.
The eaves didn't come down most of the way
to the ground; there was a decent-sized wall, too high
for most things to scale. But I get the next bit right:
it was late, very late; we'd been all the way to
Paris and back; not set off until after lunch, parked
the car on a housing estate in the suburbs, got the
train in, had a meal on the Left Bank,
taunted a police van of scoundrels,
marvelled at the smart cars of St Germaine, caught the
dernier Metro, been stranded in a ghetto, somehow
found our way back to the car, driven to
Normandy in the early hours, seen a
fox on the road, and arrived
exhausted, craving sleep in the gîte.

You take over because, for reasons that will become clear,
I don't have first-hand experience of the finer details.
Hadn't been in bed more than five minutes, you say,
when we heard it: it was padding across the roof and it was
heavy, about the weight of a man. We'd just
bolted the shutters and it was coming
down to each one in turn. You'd seen too many
horror films. I, however, had seen very few; didn't know
if this was in the plot or not, instantly fell asleep. Which
was probably an instinctively animalistic thing to do. Next
morning I was still alive and so were you but you'd had
considerably less sleep. Remains to this day a
mystery. Useful as a late-night tale—and as a
demonstration of my power of slumber.

Conversation Piece

Outside the factory where they make
tubular steel furniture,
the chairs of a tubular green dining set
are deep in conversation
in the long grass
by the gate.

The Last of the Hares

I remember a grim night when we saw one
a long way off, in a rut on the rifle range,
with its ears long and low just below the wind;
we had to look again to make sure it wasn't just
a rut. And then on the hill, when a dog disturbed
a patch of gorse and had to be pulled back from
the leverets. Other dogs did for them though.
The last I heard was of one howling like a child,
when it was caught by its feet in strawberry netting.

The Nina Sequence

i.

Nina Has a Zen Mind

Nina has a Zen mind.
In the park, which is just the park,
she sees our dog, which is just a dog.
When she sees our dog,
she doesn't think of other
dogs she has known;
she has known
no other dogs.
She knows our dog and
can just about say its name.
She sees
our dog.

I watch her absorbed in the act of
looking at our dog.
Her mind isn't wandering
to other dog moments;
she isn't thinking that
this is a wonderful thing to
do, this looking at this dog;
she isn't thinking that this
is such a wonderful thing to do
but it isn't going to last
and that this first day of spring
is really another day closer
to next winter. She
doesn't know winter. She

doesn't know spring.
She doesn't know past.
She doesn't know now or later.
She doesn't know knowing.
She knows our dog.
She's just looking at our dog.

ii.

The Dog, the Baby and the Ball

The dog approaches the ball
as if it were something living.
She is suspicious of its cheerful stripes,
outraged by its effortless movement.
The baby, who is happy simply to
marvel at it, is delighted by
the dog's antagonism. She
flops down on her nappy and
gets her hands ready to clap.
When at last the dog corners
the invader between a plant pot
and the wall the baby shuffles up to her,
puts a hand on her shoulder
and together they stare,
wondering what this thing
will do next.

iii.

Learning to Talk

Nina talks with the only equipment
she has for now.

She has four teeth—
two up; two down;
she pushes breath against them,
through them,
to form an eloquent happy hiss.

And through her untuned voice box
she forces her thoughts,
lets her tongue
splash about in them;
dipping in and out of the flow,
it shapes her song into an
almost-yodel.
You can feel her little
voice muscles flex
inside her cardigan.

iv.

For Nina (But Also for Jasmine and Rosie)

First day of December,
our shadows on stilts,
yours dancing at the end
of my sun-stretched arm.

Spring by the Side of the Lake

Lacking the aerodynamic properties of day-old
bread and tasting as bad as it looked
the biscuit and green marshmallow creation proved
to be not much use for eating or throwing.
It lay on the boards of the little jetty,
and quickly began its work of turning the wood
the colour of neglected copper. You used a twig
to get it to the water, scraping it between the gaps.
Below, where the lake floor was mainly concrete and
very old loaf, the carp stirred themselves from their
yeasty torpor, rippled the surface with their mouths and
curious barbels. But even they were not in the mood
for our viridian Easter offering.

On Spurn Head

Along the sands that swallowed villages
I looked for bits of our cliff,
carried south by long-shore drift,
and found instead a lost housing estate
where a lifeboat crew, waiting for the call,
drank beer and barbecued,
and a long-suffering man
at a charity stall
sold detective novels
and crossword anthologies
from a caravan.

August Alpaca

It is August bank holiday in England.
It is raining; we are autumn inside. Inside
we are also bicarby scones and powdered
coffee. We can see our faces in the picnic

benches. I have been to the car to get winter
layers. The abandoned diggers on the temporary
beach look like sad birds. No one
is bouncing on the bouncy castle. The animal

petting tent contains no one except
petting animals. Deep in the marquee
the balloon bender looks deflated. On the bypass
the caravans are going home.

In the middle of the field there are two wet
alpacas. One is getting flighty and is
edging towards his Anderson shelter. The other
is a Zen master. He

scrutinises the middle distance. Is unmoved
by the rain on his eyelashes.

The Christmas Ships

Out past the priory they
lounge at anchor,
big-bellied and hungry for cars.

Our pretend spruce should be visible
from their high decks and at night
they are lit up like trees
but they don't make a big thing of it.

On Christmas Eve the satellite watched them
cruising empty down the Baltic; at New Year
it'll track them full to Ijmuiden or St Petersburg.

I stare at them through binoculars,
trying to catch a glimpse of turkey or crackers.

The Last Metro

There's a fight on the platform.
When our train arrives it
conveniently provides another
arena for it and it staggers in—
some arms and screams
and stuff—then staggers off,
pulling with it an entourage of
gawkers who get as far as
the sliding doors then slink back.

The Kindness of Strangers

We swim to the mouth of the bay,
you with bite-sized bits of toffee
carried inventively in the jam jar of your goggles.
You give me the goggles to wear then
cast the toffee on the ocean.
All I can see are drops of water on the plastic,
but it feels like I'm in someone's pond.
There are muscular fish between my legs.
They are happy fish.

That night,
over a relaxing drink at the hotel,
the proprietor says he thinks
toffee makes fish go blind.

Stockpiling *Weetabix*

Every day at 9.28 he turns
the corner, making steady, sensible
progress in his *Clark's* shoes,
with his two carrier bags of groceries:
one day *Asda*, the next *Marks & Spencer*,
and each day crammed with the same things:
a box of *Weetabix*, packets of this and that,
tins, cartons—stuff that will make it really
hard to climb the hill with legs that
must have done 80 years at least.
What does he do with it all?
What does he know that we don't?

I picture him with his neat attentive wife,
settling down for a cup of tea and a golden
oldies programme on local radio, having shut a door
on the biggest stockpile of provisions this side
of the Whitehall bunkers.

Don't Bother the Boa

They don't want to get Monty frisky
so he's only fed his defrosted rats
once a week or so. In the meantime
he spends his days digesting lukewarm rodents
and sloughing off his skin.
If they unconstricted this boa
he'd reach from the fire escape to the display
of vintage chocolate wrappers, they say.
But the blokes who make sure that
no one releases the tarantulas into
the reproduction Victorian café
are not about to demonstrate the truth
of their thought-provoking claim.
Slumped in their plastic stacking chairs
in the mock tropics of the museum
they are as sluggish as their reptiles.

An Unfeasible Amount of Chewing Gum

They assumed it was chewing gum
and at first we thought that too,
only it occurred to us eventually that there'd have to be
an unfeasible amount of chewing
to produce this amount of chewing gum.

There would have to be a town
of aching-jawed folk masticating
day and night; trucks would have to be queuing
up at newsagents and garages to maintain
the steady flow of *Airwaves* and *Juicy Fruit*.

It turned out to be comparably
indefatigable lichen, doing lichenous things
between the filaments of the tarmac
and the invisibly abrasive surface of the
park pavements, undeterred and apparently
not disheartened when we trample what
most still assume to be dried gum.

Elegance

When he orders his *grande latte*
she tries to sell him a supplementary apricot croissant.
On the dark wood shelves behind her
cans of lemonade are arranged so as to
make him think he is somewhere foreign;
the cabinet on the counter displays
triple Belgian chocolate muffins and artfully wrapped
Italian cakes that are not obviously meant for eating;
the individual pecan pies look unreal, they are so
perfect.

He takes his *latte* outside, where they have attempted
to establish cafe society opposite *Shoe Zone* and
Fawcett's Quality Butchers.
He has a paper cup of iced water—
a nice continental touch, that. He sets it down with his
coffee at one of the little metal tables
and eases his tracksuited bulk on to a chair;
his right leg begins to twitch excitedly.
From a supermarket carrier bag he pulls out
pea pods—and begins shelling.

It Was in a Municipal Swimming Pool
Near Teddington

It was in a municipal swimming pool near Teddington
that I met a Caucasian whose hair was
curlier than mine. After he'd told me how he'd done it,
I breaststroked distractedly and at the end of the next
length grazed my nose on the lip of the deep end.

He said he'd used fabric conditioner, so
I bought some at the VG, rubbed it in,
then went for another swim. Afterwards,
as I balanced on one sock in the changing rooms,
I realised my locks had turned to knots.

As we ran our fingers through our (own)
tresses in the pub across the road, he pointed out
a woman sitting in the corner. He told me
that it was Twinkle who in 1964 had had a hit with *Terry*,
(although sometimes, in the telling, I get those names
confused).

That night we played *Alison* by Elvis Costello,
and he showed me his *Moby Dick* (an old
Penguin copy—this is not a poem about
homosexual revelation).

Thelonious Monk

Bent over the piano,
lampshade on your head,
you are looking for notes
you lost down the cracks
between the keys.

Alternative Obituary

Ralph Coates and Captain Beefheart died the same day.
One was a winger famed for his comb-over—
he played for Burnley, Spurs and England;
the other was an anarchic avant-garde rock singer.

Beefheart made his debut for the claret and blues in 1961,
being appointed captain the following year.

Frank Blunstone's Teeth

Most days they worked on buttermilk
and colcannon. Nothing too taxing, although
they would have been up for steak. Didn't
contribute to too many smiles either,
but once in a while they'd catch the light
from the lough and the old guy could've done
one half of a toothpaste advert. Nobody
remembers precisely how they came to be his.
Inevitably legends built up. Some say
they were rushed back still warm, almost,
and delivered the day after the match;
others that they returned, in time, with young Johnny
who'd won them in a card game in Kilburn.
Either way, they've been transferred now.
Extracted unceremoniously when he died,
they were last sighted, unlabelled,
in a box of pipes at the house sale.

In his autobiography the great Stanley Matthews tells the story of
Chelsea and England footballer Frank Blunstone losing his top set of
dentures in the excitement of watching Tommy Taylor score a goal for
England against Ireland at Wembley in 1957. According to Sir Stanley,
the teeth fell six or seven rows down the Wembley stands and were never
retrieved, but fellow footballer Jimmy McIlroy reckoned he met a man
in County Cork who was still wearing them years later.

An Ode to the Aptly Named Patricia on the Occasion of Her 70th Birthday

You're a shy lass hiding inside a hardcase,
you're a slyly maternal paedophobe,
you're a stoic who cries at choirs;
you don't talk about love because
talk is cheap, but you dish it out
like it's one of your tinned-fruit flans.

You'd be more comfortable with vacuum-sealed aliens,
but you accommodated gerbils and a poodle,
and would have got the car out for them in the
middle of the night, as you would for your grandchildren,
or anyone else's grandchildren, and picked them up
from the north of Scotland or the south of France,

which act is the equivalent of hearts and flowers
to you, but you don't talk about it because
talk is cheap, and in your case mostly fast,
and loud and loose, particularly in places
where it is meant to be slow and quiet and circumspect,
which is all it needs to be for you to hear it

through walls; and sometimes you communicate
in Morse with your fingers and feet,
and have to pour your talk into crochet strokes,
because other humans are too slow,
when they wear their hearts on their sleeve
and talk about flowers, which you prefer in clinical beds
or non-drip vases where they can pit their scent against

Domestos. I could say we wouldn't want you to change,
but talk is cheap and we know you couldn't
even if you or we wanted because, as you always say,
leopards don't change their spots.
We could give you hearts and flowers, but actually
they're not that cheap, so here are a few blunt words.

Budapest Morning

Light on in the light,
rain on the elder,
a dog barks; on the chest of drawers,
a patient television;
somewhere a hinge
twitches like a cooling stove.

Zoo Café in the Storm

Rain hits the pavement
like carp biting the surface of a pond.
On the terrace that was meant
to make a feature of outside,
only inside is practical:
the classical staircase
leads to deeper wet.
Scooters rev, horns sound,
trees glisten like crocodiles.

Come Dine With Me

Come Dine With Me is not
about competitive cooking. It's
about God. It confirms that he is invisible
but all-seeing and, as I suspected, very
sarky. He is not a patient god. He is not a tolerant
god. He sees the faults in our little plans,
our ill-thought-out itineraries and, most of all,
our recipes. He does not hold back. He does not
hold his tongue. He makes jokes at our expense.
And he cracks them with other invisible, all-seeing
beings.

Come Dine With Me confirms a lot of the stuff in
the Bible. He meant that bit about Pride.
If we find our little jokes amusing, or we think our
decor is cool, he will smite us without mercy. He is
also cuttingly disdainful of those who think
great riches will inevitably be theirs. Much
of the New Testament material is, however, revealed to be
wishful thinking. God is particularly down on the meek,
and the naff (although the latter are not specified in
traditional versions of the Beatitudes).

Come Dine With Me is not
about competitive cooking. It
just looks like it is. That's the clever
thing. If it was billed as a programme about
religion, we'd switch over to watch a
crappy reality show instead.

Dawdon Colliery

In the summer of '76
it was also hot
underground; it was also hot
below the ground
below the water.

We went down in a lift
from the top of the
grass, took a train
out towards Denmark.

Beneath the seabed
we found a room, low-roofed,
where a man lay on his side
hanging on to something the size
of an Austin *Allegro*, which he was
crashing into the walls.

We stood there watching,
with the wind ruffling our hair
below the ground
below the water.

Archaeology

Next to the dig
outside the railings of the Roman fort
archaeology continues—
even on Sundays.

They are excavating the cracks
between the pavements,
piling high the soil.
Sometimes you'll see the workers
emerging busy from the ground.

Back at the fort
the polythene protective covering flutters.
The bells ring at the Mission
across the road.

The Wall

The wall looks at me
as I stand there
waiting for the dog to pee.
I am excited by the scent of spring;
on the bend of its lane it has been doing this
spring thing for years,
this archetype of brick boundary work,
this mother of all walls. It has seen it all.

Up by its chest
it has bellied out with the weight of the world.
It has had other walls and times stitched to it,
some with just a line of mortar,
some grafted course by course.
Here's the scar of a coal house,
there an outside bog. Jesus, those look like
arrow slits near the top!

This is no fancy thing.
It wasn't supposed to be here still.
These bricks are seconds, thirds,
not even proper brick shape down the bottom;
most are kiln-burnt;
all are smoke-grimed.
But it's here.
Looking at me as I wait for the dog
and think of spring.

Crustaceans

You have to prise them out of their shells;
they are secretive and look as though they secrete;
they are little muscular creatures,
the colour of slime and old blood.
Roasted pistachios are shellfish for vegetarians.

Ninety-Nine Per Cent of All Known Germs

I am the one per cent of all known germs
disinfectants never touch.
I laugh in the face of *Dettol*,
I gargle with *Domestos*.
On your work surfaces
and under the rim of your
toilet bowls I bask.
You'll never catch me.

A Golden Oriel in the Orchard

They're hard to spot even when you're not
weeping. Shy and high-flying, they offer only
a flash of yellow within the canopy green. A crick
comes with the territory, unless you're on apple-picking
ladders, but then you'd scare the bird.

But with tears—particularly those that blur the mind's
eye, when you're on a bench near a station, say, or
looking along the line of carriages, and memories are
stirred of that last picnic beneath the ripening Granny
Smiths—it's easy to lose your ornithological
perspicacity. It's easy to confuse one with a *Bullock's* or
a *Hooded*, or, more likely—if you've got a song driving
you to distraction—Hoagy Carmichael's *Baltimore*.

Afterwards you could kick yourself, at the twitchers'
convention, when you pick up your tote bag
and pin on your society button, and with the upset
receding down the track you swap lists of recent
sightings, including the *Golden* you saw or kind of saw
among the apple trees of your mind, and that know-all
from the Audubon says surely you mean *Icterus spurius*,
the *Orchard*, because the *Golden*'s never been spotted in
North America. That is mortifying enough, but then
he points out: 'And it's oriole, not oriel. An oriel
is a small room with a polygonal window.' And
once again you sit down and weep.

The title is a line, supplied at random, from the text of Elizabeth
Smart's By Grand Central Station I Sat Down and Wept.

Bird Listening

I used to watch birds,
but it became so dull.
I yearned for mystery, adventure.
I took up bird listening.
Oh, that's been done, I hear you say.
You can buy long-playing records full of birdsong.
Quite so. But birdsong is so easy to capture.
The bird is a natural Caruso;
it needs no encouragement to warble.
No. I listen for bird breath.
I go out into the great silent aviary
of the night with nothing more than
a gramophone trumpet, needle and wax cylinder.
In the hours before the dawn chorus
I sit under trees and just listen.
Got nothing yet but I know the little
blighters are out there.

The Return of the Wildwood

Next to a *Monster Munch* packet
in a crack in the concrete of a wet yard
a sycamore seedling gathers nutrients
from the grunge, forces its roots beneath
the foundations of a house and cracks the walls.

On the pitches the rain that used to dilute
the washday soap in that dank gap,
falls unlamented. The ragwort follows
and the cottage-garden strays, and the dock
and the wormwood, racing the seeding turf,
now not so confident of its grassy dominion.

In a potting shed, seed trays overflow;
a forsythia, tired of waving at the window,
rises through the boards. A lawn rake falls.
So much compost! So much sun
for the elbowing victors! How giddy we would
have been with all this oxygen.

Where we saw chimneypots and lamp posts,
the rooks never stopped seeing trees.

On the Frontier

From my window they looked like
carvings in light wood,
gentle against the sky.
Through binoculars they turned out
to be cat and bird skulls,
nailed totem-style
over his dog pens.

Soon he came to tell me
about the terns and skuas;
how the terns would
push sprat to the surface,
but the skuas would be waiting,
and they'd give them
a fucking body-blow.
If they didn't drop the fish
the skuas would eat them as well.

In his garden
he was the skua.
He'd wait for the cats
to come for the greenfinch,
then spear them
with a sharpened fork shaft
and string them up.

At sea it was the seals.
*You know a seal has to eat
a third of its own weight a day
to stay alive,* he'd tell me.

Well, if it weighs a ton,
that's a helluva lot of fish.
It's not right if you've got to compete
with an animal to make your living.

If he saw a seal family
as he pushed out past the rocks,
he'd shoot the pups
and feed them to his dogs
He'd have eaten them himself
if he could've *stood the salt*.

The Sea

It was like we had a dragon
at the end of our fields
that roared a lot and
needed appeasing.

My grandmother used to point to a lady
in the cake shop, whose son,
she said, had been killed by it
when swimming with friends.

This could have been a lie;
grandma was fond of a cautionary
untruth. But I would stand and stare
at the cake lady's cheerfulness
and marvel at the healing power
of cakes.

My dad—and his dad before him—
used to say: *If you come back drowned,*
I'll kill you.
We never gave reason for such tautological slaughter,
but sometimes
we didn't all come back together.

Once, a boy fell from a cliff—
not a very high one—and we ran
to get his dad, who was about 8ft tall
and had a quiff like Freddie Trueman's.
He set off on foot, with us scurrying after.

At first we thought he was going to belt
us for being unscathed.
Then we asked him if
he was going to thump his son
for being so stupid.
When he said no, it came to us.
As he rolled up his sleeves
and we turned back
we decided that at last,
the dragon was going to get it.

Potato Picking With Our Dodgy Neighbour

He had a go-cart, made from planks
and pram wheels, and I sat on it with
the sacks. There were many of us;
I might as well say we sang as we went.
The field was in front of two rows of
houses: you stepped across the pavement
into a ploughed field and we worked there for an hour
or two after tea, grubbing around for left-over
potatoes until the light went.

When we got back, thirsty,
he produced a bottle of lemonade that turned out
to be turps.

I Grew Up in the Land
Before Yoghurt

I grew up in the land before yoghurt,
we kept our milk in a red plastic bucket.
The water in the bucket kept the thick milk
cold, except when it didn't. Then we threw it
down the sink. Never occurred to us
to add raspberries.

The Capsicum's Arrival

It was shortly before adulthood
that I first encountered
a pepper.

Prior to that I'd been acquainted with pepper,
a beige culinary powder
favoured by grown-ups.

In the Old Days

Everything was better, they say.
Portions were bigger,
people whiter;
flavours were blander,
lyrics clearer;
days were longer,
life was safer;
men were grander,
women tamer;
the fat were fat,
the weak were meek;
there was a definite shape
to the working week.

I say: *thank the lord we live now.*

I Spy the Unusual

Forty points for a front room,
kept for best, and a range
of cut-glass vases, displayed therein.
Allow yourself another ten if viewed
through a bow window in the rain.

Fifty points if you spot a man
below middle-age with a comb-over;
twenty for a reindeer design
zip-up woollen cardigan.
Put the two together,
get an extra five, providing they're not
being sported ironically.

Look out for an elderly geezer
wearing a tie on a summer's day,
that'll bump up your score.
Ditto for a Mark 2 Cortina
being driven by someone other
than a classic car enthusiast.

Keep your ears peeled
for any mention of Eamonn Andrews
and your eyes for
a mobile butcher's shop.
Help yourself to
as many as you like if you find a town
where they still have half-day closing.

Curling the Foolscap

We knew there was no hope for us
when the Grim Reaper came for
Aunty Olive.

Immortality's best hope
would belt down to the pound shops
every morning,
looking 37 at 88. Then

belt back for piano lessons;
gave her last one 65 years after
the first, a week before the
end, ruling out the lines of the stave
with a vehemence that
curled the foolscap.

Acknowledgements

Some of the poems in this collection have appeared in *By Grand Central Station We Sat Down and Wept* (Red Squirrel Press, 2010) and *Double Bill* (forthcoming from Red Squirrel Press, October 2014).

Alistair Robinson is married with three daughters and lives in South Shields. He is a senior lecturer in journalism at the University of Sunderland. His chapbook *South of Souter* (Sand) was published in 2003. The following year he won a Northern Promise Award from New Writing North. His collection *Stereograms of the Dead* (Red Squirrel Press) was published in 2009. Alistair is the author of two books on theatre history and one on the history of Sunderland. He also works as a musician. His jazz trio, the *Bicycle Thieves*, plays at venues all over the North East of England and has released *Stolen Moments* on Road Goes On Forever Records. Alistair's compositions for that album were published in the USA by Bug Music.